T is for Tortilla

A SOUTHWESTERN ALPHABET BOOK

By
JODY ALPERS

Illustrated By
CELESTE JOHNSON

*Best Wishes
Jody Alpers
1996*

To Helen:
Always an encourager, always a friend.

In Memory:
Kristi and Kristi Rose

Thank you:
Jesus, Greg, Kyle, Kim, Emily,
Sue Sue & Clyde

PUBLISHED BY FRY-INNOVATIONS

Contact:
Libros de Niños
2505 N. Washington
Roswell, New Mexico 88201
Fax (505) 622-8473

THIRD PRINTING AUGUST 1996

This alphabet book tells of many things found in the Southwest. Some of the words in the book are Spanish or Indian words so we have made "helper words" to help you learn how to say them. Have fun learning new alphabet words from the Southwest!

Adobe (uh-DOH-bee)
Burro (boor -oh)
Cowboy
Desert
Ewe (you)
Fiesta (fee-yes-ta)
Guitar
Hacienda (ah-see-en-da)
Indian Culture
Jackrabbit
Kerchief
Luminarias (loo-meen-AHR-ee ahs)
Mesa

New Mexico
Ollas (Oh-yahs)
Piñata (pen-ya tuh)
Quarter Horse
Roadrunner
Sunset
Tortilla (TOR-tee-ya)
Uno (oo-no)
Vigas (VEE-gahs)
Windmill
Xeric (Zee-rik)
Yucca (yuk-uh)
Zia (Zee-uh)

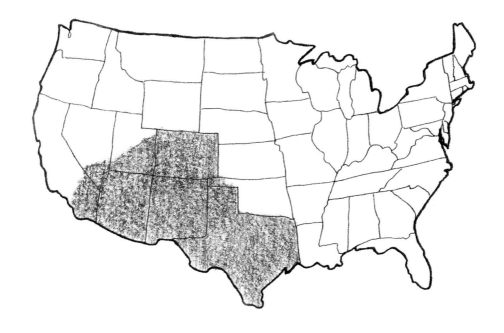

The shaded areas on this United States
map are the states in the Southwest. Do
you live in the Southwest?

is for Adobe (uh **DOH** bee)

Have you ever heard of a house made of mud? In the Southwest many houses and buildings are made of adobe. Bricks are made by mixing mud and straw. The mud is poured into molds to be dried in the sun. The mud bricks are used to build buildings. Would you like to live in a house made of mud?

 is for Burro (boor-oh)

A burro is a small donkey which is sometimes used as a pack animal. A pack animal carries things on his back. People can ride on the burro's back too. Burros have long ears and shaggy coats. Can you think of other animals that carry things or people on their backs?

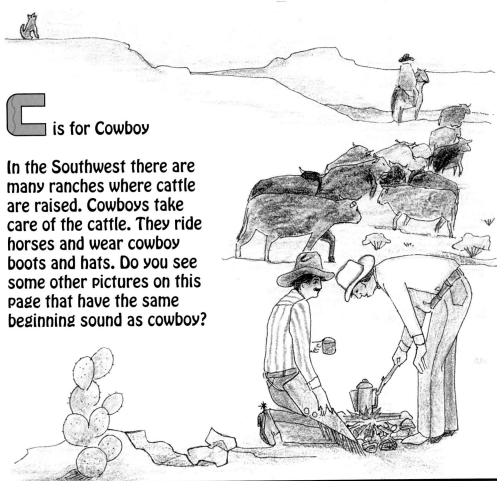

C is for Cowboy

In the Southwest there are many ranches where cattle are raised. Cowboys take care of the cattle. They ride horses and wear cowboy boots and hats. Do you see some other pictures on this page that have the same beginning sound as cowboy?

is for Desert

A desert is a place where it doesn't rain much. Not many plants can grow in the desert because it is so dry. Cactus live in the desert. Can you see some other plants and animals that live in the desert?

E is for Ewe (you)

A ewe is a mother sheep. Some ranches in the Southwest raise sheep instead of cattle. Sheep are raised for their meat and wool. How many ewe's have baby lambs in this picture?

F is for Fiesta (fee-yes-ta)

A Spanish word for a party or celebration is a fiesta. Usually a band plays and people dance. Food is served and sometimes people play games. Maybe you could call your next party a fiesta.

 is for Guitar

A guitar is a flat musical instrument with a long neck. It usually has six strings which are strummed with the fingers. Sometimes western singers play the guitar. Have you ever played a guitar?

is for Hacienda (ah-see-en-da)

Hacienda is a Spanish word for house. A hacienda is usually a large house. There is a song called "My Adobe Hacienda." Can you guess what the house in the song was made of?

is for Indian Culture

There are different tribes of the American Indians in the Southwest. Many things today in the Southwest are from the Indian's way of life. Some Indian customs the Southwest enjoys are: food, art, music and language. This picture shows an Indian woman weaving a rug.

J is for Jackrabbit

A jackrabbit has long ears and can run fast. They are easy to find in the Southwest because there are many of them.

K is for Kerchief

Cowboys wear kerchiefs around their necks to keep off the sun. Sometimes, to keep from breathing too much dust, they pull it up over their nose. You can make your own cowboy kerchief by folding a square scarf or bandana into a triangle and tying it over your nose.

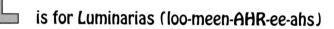 is for Luminarias (loo-meen-AHR-ee-ahs)

A luminaria is a Christmas decoration of the Southwest. They are made with brown paper sacks filled half way with sand and a small candle is placed inside. The sacks are used to line the roof (usually a flat-top roof) of a house or building. When the candles are lit, it makes a pretty decoration. The tradition is the tiny lights light the way for the Christ Child. There are other names for luminarias too.

 is for Mesa

A mesa is a mountain which is different than any other type of mountain because it is flat on top with steep rock sides. Some people call this a table-top mountain because they think it looks like a table. Would you like to try to climb a mesa? Do you think it would be easy?

is for New Mexico

New Mexico is the 47th state. Some people think New Mexico is still in Old Mexico and do not know it is in the United States, but it is. New Mexico is the fifth largest state. Can you find it on the map in the front of this book?

is for Ollas (Oy-yas)

Ollas are Indian water pots. The Pueblo Indians used to keep their drinking water in these pots. They did not move around like the Plains Indians did so they could have many big pots and bowls. Why do you think the Plains Indians did not have many big pots and bowls?

P is for Piñata (pen-ya-tuh)

A piñata is used for parties or fiestas. It is a paper maché figure covered with brightly colored tissue paper. In the middle of the figure is a small clay pot filled with candy or small toys. Children take turns being blindfolded and try to break the piñata using a stick. When the piñata breaks, all the children scramble to get the prizes. Do you think it would be fun to try to break a piñata?

is for Quarter Horse

Many cowboys of the Southwest ride quarter horses because they are strong, quick and can turn fast. This helps the cowboy when he has to work cattle. The quarter horse got his name because he is fast in the quarter mile race.

 is for Roadrunner

A roadrunner is a type of bird found in the Southwest. He would rather run than fly. The roadrunner's favorite foods are mice and rattlesnakes. People in the Southwest like it when a roadrunner lives near their house. Can you guess why?

S is for Sunset

The Southwest is known for its beautiful sunsets. Often in the evenings, as the sun sets in the West, there will be many beautiful colors. This is called a sunset. Many people think the sunsets in the Southwest are some of the most beautiful in the world. Can you name some of the colors in this picture of a sunset?

T is for Tortilla (tor-tee-uh)

A tortilla is a type of Mexican bread, it does not come in a loaf like other bread. It is flat and round and cooked on both sides. They can be made from flour or corn. Tortillas are used in many different Mexican dishes or eaten plain. Have you ever eaten a tortilla?

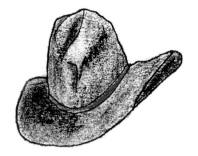

 is for Uno (oo-no)

Uno is the Spanish word for the number one. Can you count how many things on these pages have uno?

 is for Vigas (Vee-gahs)

A viga is a long piece of wood used to hold up a roof or ceiling in an adobe house. Sometimes a viga is so long that it sticks out to the outside of a house. How many vigas do you see in this ceiling?

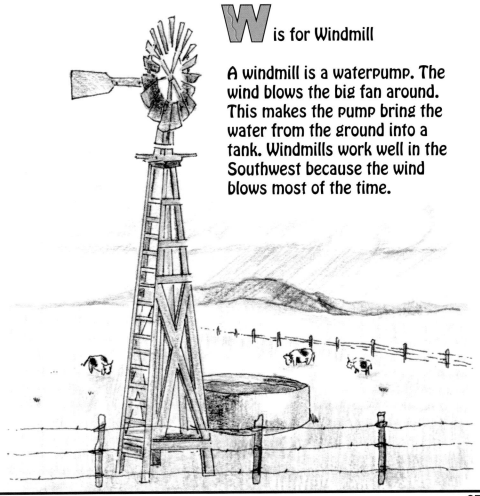

W is for Windmill

A windmill is a waterpump. The wind blows the big fan around. This makes the pump bring the water from the ground into a tank. Windmills work well in the Southwest because the wind blows most of the time.

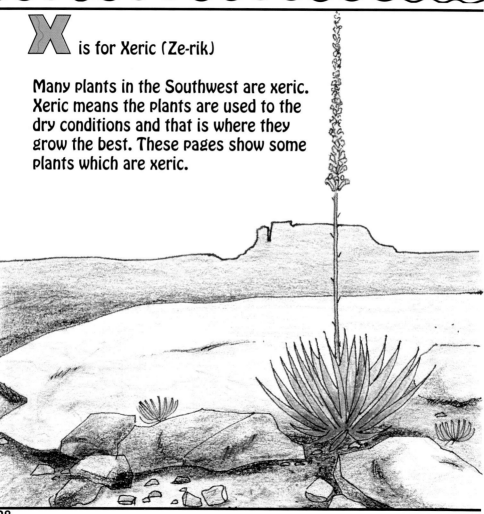

X is for Xeric (Ze-rik)

Many plants in the Southwest are xeric. Xeric means the plants are used to the dry conditions and that is where they grow the best. These pages show some plants which are xeric.

Y is for Yucca (yuk-uh)

A yucca is one type of plant that likes dry heat. Instead of having leaves, this plant has sharp spines. It has pretty yellow flowers. Can you guess how this plant got the nick-name "the Spanish Sword"?

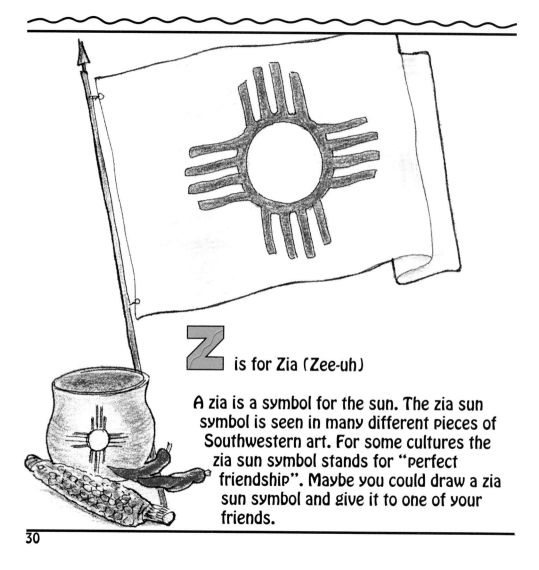

Z is for Zia (Zee-uh)

A zia is a symbol for the sun. The zia sun symbol is seen in many different pieces of Southwestern art. For some cultures the zia sun symbol stands for "perfect friendship". Maybe you could draw a zia sun symbol and give it to one of your friends.